Sounds All Around Us

Sound and Hearing

Catherine Veitch

www.raintreepublishers.co.uk
Visit our website to find out more information about Raintree books.

To order:
☎ Phone 0845 6044371
🖨 Fax +44 (0) 1865 312263
💻 Email myorders@capstonepub.co.uk

Customers from outside the UK please telephone +44 1865 312262

Raintree is an imprint of Capstone Global Library Limited, a company incorporated in England and Wales having its registered office at 7 Pilgrim Street, London, EC4V 6LB – Registered company number: 6695582

Text © Capstone Global Library Limited
First published in hardback in 2009
Paperback edition first published in 2010

Edited by Charlotte Guillain, Rebecca Rissman, and Catherine Veitch
Designed by Joanna Hinton-Malivoire
Original illustrations © Capstone Global Library Ltd 2008
Illustrations: Tony Wilson (p. 16)
Picture research by Tracy Cummins
Originated by Heinemann Library
Printed by Leo Paper Group

ISBN 978 0 431 19392 2 (hardback)
13 12 11 10 09
10 9 8 7 6 5 4 3 2 1

ISBN 978 0 431 19398 4 (paperback)
14 13 12 11 10
10 9 8 7 6 5 4 3 2 1

British Library Cataloguing in Publication Data
Veitch, Catherine
Sound and hearing. - (Sounds all around us)
534
A full catalogue record for this book is available from the British Library.

Acknowledgements
The author and publisher are grateful to the following for permission to reproduce copyright material: Agefotostock pp. **18 left** (©Bilderlounge), **19 left** (©zefa RF); Alamy pp. **6 left** (©Massive Pixels /Robert Ashton), **10 right** (©Images of Africa Photobank), **13 right** (©Anna Sherwin); AP Photo pp. **21 right** (©The Superior Daily Telegram/Jamey Penney); Getty Images **pp. 4** (©Anthony Plummer), **5 left** (©Alex Mares-Manton), **6 right** (©Livia Corona), **11 left** (©Jose Luis Pelaez Inc), **12 left** (©Terry Vine), **13 left** (©DAJ), **17 left** (©Purestock), **17 right** (©Bob Stefko), **19 right** (©Geri Lavrov), **20 left** (©Photo and Co), **22 bottom right** (©Penny Tweedie); istockphoto pp. **22 top right** (©Liza McCorkle), **22 bottom left** (©Cliff Parnell); Jupiter Images pp. **11 right** (©BananaStock), **14** (©Hemera Technologies); Landov p. 8 (©ITAR-TASS/Valery Matytsin); Photolibrary p. **15** (©age fotostock/ Bartomeu Amengual); Richard Levine p. **18 right** (©Richard Levine); Shutterstock pp. 5 right (©Christine Gonsalves), **7** (©Lane V. Erickson), **9** (©Neale Cousland), **10 left** (©gemphotography), **12 right** (©Jan van der Hoeven), 20 right (©Jerry Horbert), **22 top left** (©kristian sekulic); Visuals Unlimited p. **21 left** (©Visuals Unlimted).

Cover photograph of people watching a performer from Africa reproduced with permission of Getty Images (©AFP Photo/TEH ENG KOON).
Back cover photographs: a drumstick striking a Celtic bohdran drum reproduced with permission of Jupiter Images (©Hemera Technologies); a roaring lion reproduced with permission of Shutterstock (©Kristian Sekulic).

The publishers would like to thank Nancy Harris and Adriana Scalise for their assistance in the preparation of this book.

Every effort has been made to contact copyright holders of material reproduced in this book. Any omissions will be rectified in subsequent printings if notice is given to the publishers.

Contents

Some words are shown in bold, **like this.** They are explained in "Words to know" on page 23.

Let's look at sound

There are many different sounds in the world around us. Sounds come from many places. We hear sounds with our ears.

We like to hear some sounds. We do not like to hear other sounds. Which sounds do you like to hear? Which sounds do you not like to hear?

Loud and quiet sounds

Some sounds are loud. Loud sounds can be heard from far away. These sounds get louder the nearer you get to them. How does it feel to hear a very loud sound?

Some sounds are quiet. Quiet sounds can only be heard from nearby. Can you make a quiet sound?

High and low sounds

Some sounds are high. A whistle makes a high sound.
When we listen to high and low sounds, we hear
different **pitches**. A whistle's sound has a high pitch.

Some sounds are low. A lawnmower makes a low sound. A lawnmower's sound has a low pitch.

Sounds our bodies make

We can use our bodies to make different sounds.
We can shout to make a loud sound. We can blow
to make a quiet sound. We can clap our hands or
stamp our feet to make loud or quiet sounds.

We can sing to make a high sound. We can growl to make a low sound. Can you make a high sound? Can you make a low sound?

Other sounds we can make

We can make sounds with instruments. We can rattle a tambourine. We can bang a drum. Can you make a loud sound with an instrument? Can you make a quiet sound with an instrument?

We can blow a recorder. We can **pluck** a **double bass**. Can you make a high sound with an instrument? Can you make a low sound with an instrument?

What are sounds?

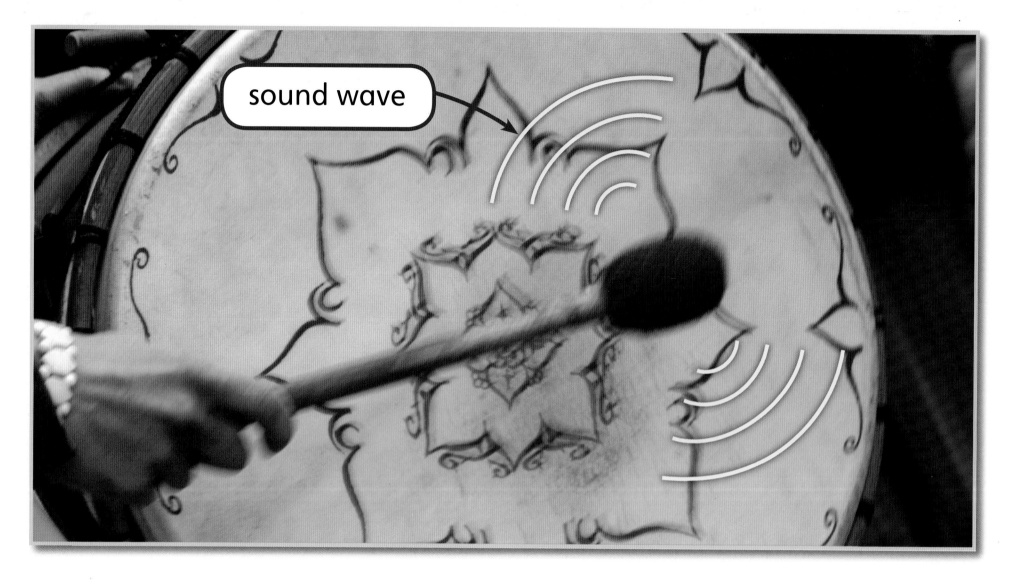

sound wave

When we make a sound we make something shake. When something shakes it **vibrates**. The air around it vibrates, too. When the air vibrates it is called a **sound wave**.

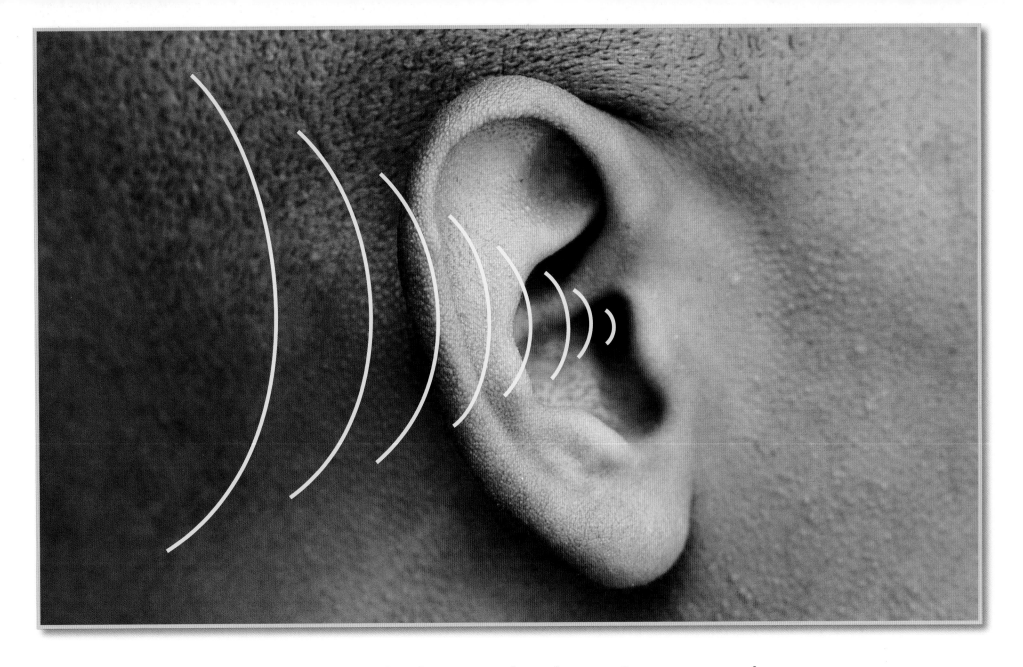

Sound waves travel through the air. Sound waves travel into our ears. Our ears are shaped like a funnel to help catch the sound waves.

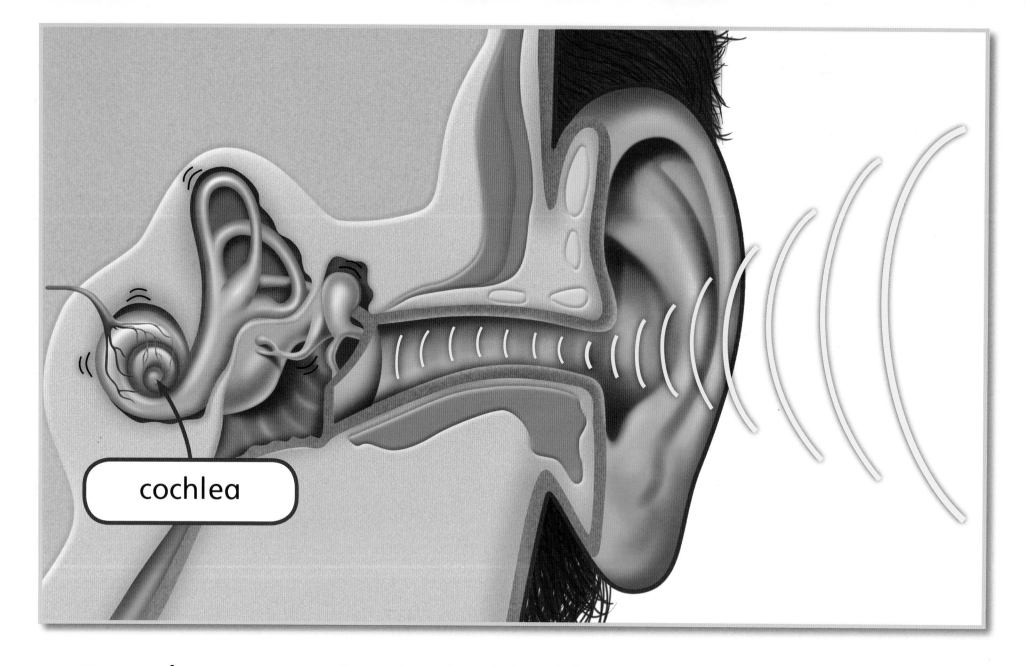

cochlea

Sound waves make the inside of our ears **vibrate**. There is a snail-shaped part inside our ear. It is called the **cochlea**. Sound waves make the cochlea vibrate. The cochlea vibrates and sends messages to our brain.

Many animals have good hearing. They can hear very quiet sounds. They can hear sounds that are far away. They have large ears to help them catch sound waves.

Sound waves can travel through objects. You can hear sounds through a woolly hat. You can hear traffic go past when you are inside a building.

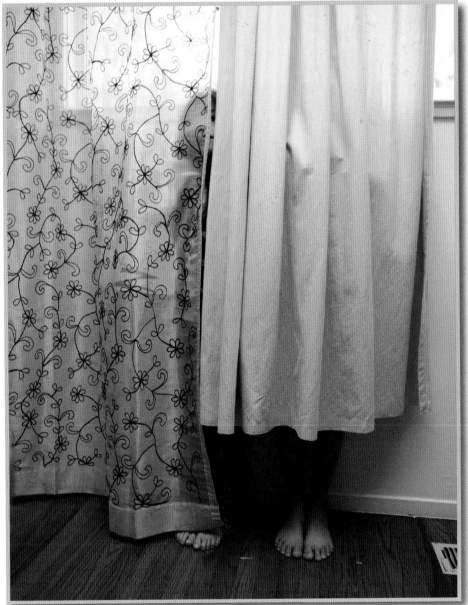

Sound waves travel through some objects more easily than others. Talk to someone through a door. Talk to someone from behind a curtain. Which object is it easier to hear through?

Sounds warn us of danger. We use our ears to listen for traffic when crossing the road. A fire alarm rings to warn us of a fire in a building.

hearing aid

Some people are **Deaf**. They may use a hearing aid to help them hear. They may make signs with their hands to communicate. This is called **sign language**.

What have you learned?

There are lots of different sounds. Can you make these sounds? Are they loud or quiet sounds? Are they high or low sounds?

Words to know

eardrum part inside your ear that shakes when sound hits it

cochlea snail-shaped part inside your ear. The cochlea shakes when sound hits it.

Deaf with little or no hearing

double bass musical instrument that looks like a large violin

pitch how high or low a sound is. A whistle makes a high sound. A whistle's sound has a high pitch.

pluck take hold of and pull something sharply. You pluck the strings of a guitar to make a sound.

sign language way to communicate using hand signals for letters or words

silence when no sound can be heard

sound wave when the air shakes very quickly

vibrate shake very quickly

Index

Note to parents and teachers

Before reading

Tell the children that we hear sounds every day. Ask them if they know how we hear sounds. Tell them that we use our ears to hear sounds. Then, together, begin creating a chart headed "Sounds and Hearing". Divide the chart into three columns, "What You Know", "What You Want to Know", and "What You Have Learned". Discuss the first two columns with the children and then fill in these columns.

After reading

• Continue discussing and filling in the chart with the children. Focus on the third column, "What You Have Learned", and ask the children what they have learned from this book.

• Vibration Experiment: Each child will need a partner and a balloon. Ask the children in their pairs to blow up a balloon, hold it against one child's ear, and have the other child speak into the balloon with their lips pressing into the balloon. Then tell the children to change over. Ask the children what they have noticed. Tell them that you can hear vibrations through the balloon and you can feel the vibrations. Remind the children that sound is created when an object and the air around it vibrates, creating sound waves.